Northern
Balcony Gardening

Brian Andrews

LONE
PINE

Homeworld

First printed in 1992   5 4 3 2 1

Printed in Canada

The Publisher:
Lone Pine Publishing
#206, 10426-81 Avenue
Edmonton, Alberta, Canada
T6E 1X5

Canadian Cataloguing in Publication Data
Andrews, Brian, 1931-
    Northern balcony gardening

(Homeworld)
ISBN 0-919433-98-7

1. Balcony gardening. I. Title. II. Series
SB419.5.A52 1992   635.9'671   C92-091197-8

Original Compilation: Keith Ashwell
Editorial: Roman Kravec
Cover Illustration: Linda Dunn
Homeworld Editor: Lloyd Dick
Printing: Friesen Printers. Altona, Manitoba, Canada

The publisher gratefully acknowledges the assistance of the Federal Department of Communications, Alberta Culture and Multiculturalism and the Alberta Foundation for the Arts in the production of this book

Contents

Balcony Gardening

There is a general trend in the world today — people are moving off the farms and into the cities. Not everyone, however, can afford a house and garden. Many people, by choice or for lack of alternatives, live in apartments, and are lucky if they have a balcony.

This book is addressed to those of you who are fortunate to have a balcony — to enable you to bring a small patch of green, of garden, back to your flat; to cheer you with the sight of green things growing outside your personal living space, living plants which can bring enjoyment to your eyes or a feast for the table.

Just as children need to learn where milk comes from, and concern about the pollution of our environment grows, so too do we need to see how plants grow, at close range. Not only does the greenery rest our eyes, but it contributes, in a small way, to the reduction of pollution, and increases our awareness of the source of our food.

If, at times, this book seems too simple for you— rejoice! You obviously have graduated to the next level of gardening, and will want to buy another in our series of **Homeworld** books, such as *Herbs*, or the complete manual by this author — *Northern Gardens.*

If, on the other hand, the book seems too technical, have patience. Consult the glossary at the back, or a good dictionary. Talk to your friendly greenhouse operator. Speak to people who have been gardening a long time. They will be only too happy to share their experience with you.

It is sometimes said that gardening is a hobby of senior citizens. Only after we have slowed down do we take up a hobby requiring such patience. To balance this view, consider that growing things requires trust in the process of life. If you are indeed an "older" person, then gardening is making the statement that you will be around long enough to enjoy the fruit of your labours. It is actually a youthful hobby, an affirmation of life!

Enjoy your balcony garden, and your new-found skill.

The Upstairs Environment

Gardens on balconies are, by definition, up in the air. As a consequence, their growing environment is different from that of their more pedestrian counterparts at ground level. Some of the factors affecting this environment include sunshine, wind, temperature, humidity, restricted soil volumes and root runs, and limited space.

The Sun's path

Generally, during mid-summer in the northern hemisphere, the sun rises in the north-east, follows an arc-shaped path — east, via the south, to west — (reaching a relatively high point above the horizon by noon) and sets in the north-west.

During mid-winter, the sun rises in the east, follows a similar but lower arc, reaches a relatively low point above the horizon by noon and sets in the west.

As a result, the warmest and sunniest balconies face south, south-west and south-east. East facing balconies are cool but receive plenty of direct sun from early morning until about 1 pm. Those facing west are very warm and sunny, receiving direct sun from mid-day until late in the evening. The coolest and shadiest balconies face north, north-east and north-west — north facing being the most shaded and cool.

Bear in mind that due to the suns path in summer, otherwise unobstructed north-facing locations receive some direct, lower-angled sun during early morning and late evening. Furthermore, if the balcony is exposed to open sky, even on the north side, the intensity of the diffused light may be relatively high. Thus, these environments may not be a gloomy as many people suppose.

Two structures which will increase shade are the roof-over, provided by the next balcony up, and the density of the surrounding barrier or railings. Similarly, adjacent apartment buildings may have a significant effect on light intensity.

Sun and heat

Heat can be reduced, and shade provided, on hot sunny balconies using screens and curtains.

Screens may be fixed or portable. They can vary in density from wide-lattice, open trellises to solid walls and fences. These may also serve to support climbing plants.

Curtains and blinds may be made of any tough, opaque material from canvas to bamboo. They can be permanently attached to, or hung by hooks from the balcony above and the railings.

Where climatically permissible, trees and shrubs in containers, and climbing plants on poles and strips of trellis may be used.

Light-coloured paints and tiles can help to reflect excessive heat.

VEGETABLES
SUN/SHADE REQUIREMENTS AND TOLERANCES

Warmest/ Sunniest	Warm/ Sunny	Sunny	Mild shade	Shaded*
cucumber	beans-bush	asparagus	chives	carrots
eggplant	beans-dry	broad beans	endive	Chinese cabbage
melons	beans-French	broccoli	kale	lettuce
peppers	beans-lima	brussels	mint	onions, bunching
squash	beans-pole	sprouts	parsley	peas
tomato	beans-soy	cauliflower	mustard	spinich
zucchini	corn	celery	greens	
	pumpkin**	garlic	turnip	
		cabbages	swiss chard	
		leek	radish	
		onion		
		parsnip		
		potato		
		rutabaga		

* Note: vegetables suitable for shade and semi-shade are also suitable for sunny-cooler locations.
** Semi-shade tolerant in warm locations.

Shade

In shady places, the light intensity can be increased by reflection. Use light-coloured paint, stains, stucco or tiles to cover the underside of upper balconies, back and side walls floors, railings and plant containers.

Fixed and portable mirrors and reflecting screens covered with aluminum foil may be used.

Solid or dense surrounding barriers can be replaced with open railings, clear plastic or safety-glass.

Supplemental lighting using fluorescent tubes and grow-lights can be installed on the underside of upper balconies, back and side walls.

Wind

Generally, the higher the balcony, the greater the wind. Depending on the height of the balcony, wind will be modified by tall trees and adjacent buildings which may have a moderating or intensifying effect.

High winds can damage plants (especially tall kinds and vines), hanging containers and portable screens.

Physiologically, especially when hot and dry, winds can cause havoc. Plants rapidly give off water vapour to the atmosphere at a rate faster than they can absorb it from the soil. This is compounded by water loss due to evaporation from the soil surface. The result is drying of the tissues and drought stress, often manifest as wilting.

Again, as suggested for providing shade, fixed or portable screens, both solid and open textured, and glass or plastic barriers may be used.

Open textured screens that allow some wind to pass through are better since they prevent severe turbulence on the leeward side of the screen. There is nothing to be gained by turning a wind problem into turbulence.

Temperature

The temperature on a balcony is a function of direct sunshine, wind, humidity, height above ground (in theory the higher, the cooler), radiant heat from the building and balcony, reflective heat and the outside temperature.

Temperature can be modified using the methods previously described for sun and shade.

Spraying the walls and floor of the balcony with cool water will also help to cool your balcony garden.

Rain

The effects of wind are compounded by lack of natural rainfall on many balconies. This results from interference by overhead balconies, side-walls and solid barriers.

Since plants are mostly in containers, window boxes and planters, their leaf canopies overhang the soil areas and shed rain onto the balcony floor where it of no benefit to the plants.

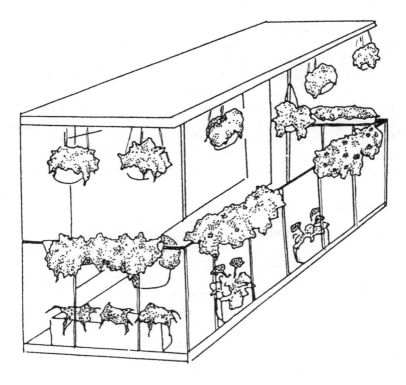

Patio pots

Also, since the total soil surface of containers and planters is relatively small, the volume of evaporation is correspondingly small—minimizing its contribution to local humidity. This is compounded by the drying effects of reflective and radiant surfaces.

Watering

Due to restricted soil volumes and the environmental factors discussed, plants dry out more quickly on balconies. Often, this is compounded by balcony gardeners being absent from home, very often at the time watering is needed.

Trickle irrigation is a system of watering slowly and continuously, drip by drip, using plastic tubes fitted with special emitters. Do-it-yourself kits are easy to obtain from most irrigation contractors and suppliers. They use little water and apply it where and when it does the most good.

Similarly, jars and cans of water with wicks or small holes provide a continuous drip on the soil surface of containers.

Wick watering involves the use of containers and planters in which fibreglass wicks are inserted into the soil mass, then threaded through the bottom of the plant container and laid in a basin or trough of water. As the plants use water, and water is lost through evaporation, the soil is kept moist through water travelling up the wick by capillary action.

Humidity

Humidity can be increased by using two inch deep trays of fine gravel with an inch of water in their bottoms from which water will continuously evaporate into the atmosphere. Plants in containers and pots may be placed on them or they can be placed on the balcony floor between or close to containers. Pieces of outdoor carpet may be dampened and similarly used.

"Damping down" or spraying the balcony floor with water will increase humidity as the water evaporates.

Misting plants with water will also help.

Water conservation

Water may be conserved in the soil, and the soil maintained in a cooler condition, by mulching. This involves placing a one inch deep layer of well-rotted manure, compost or leaf-mould, or moist peat-moss over the soil surface.

Black plastic mulch, cut to appropriate shapes to fit round the plants and their containers may also be used.

Restricted soil volumes an space

Plants on balconies in containers and planters have a restricted root-run and limited soil in which to grow. Water availability, aggravated by fast drainage and warm air temperatures, is limited — as are plant foods. Careful planning is required to maintain plant health in these confined areas.

Planning, Design and Construction

In planning and designing a balcony garden, you must face the impossibility of having the same wide range of features and plants as in a larger, ground-level garden. The key is to be selective and execute well.

A design program

The first step is to prepare a written program. This is simply a carefully worded statement of the basic functions, based on your needs and wants, that you expect the balcony garden to fulfil. It should cover such matters as sitting out, eating and drinking, entertaining, framing desirable views, need for screening, meeting environmental demands, growing vegetables (if desired), your interest level in growing plants, the

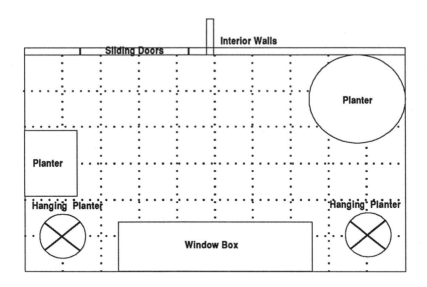

Sample site plan

time you are prepared to spend on maintenance, and in general, the kind of plants (trees, shrubs, climbers, herbaceous perennials, annuals, vegetables and fruit) you wish to grow.

Site Plan

This analysis should be followed by preparing an accurately scaled plan of the balcony on graph paper. One centimetre equals thirty centimetres would be practical and allow for all details on one plan.

Outline the shape and dimensions of the balcony, and show the exact location of back and side walls, peripheral barriers or fences, lights and electrical outlets, pillars and hose bibs, etc.

Accessibility

Analyze the accessibility of the balcony for construction purposes. Bear in mind that all construction materials, soils, plants and containers, etc. will have to be brought up from ground level via elevators, steps, hall-ways and doors. Be sure there is enough room to store and handle construction materials, on and off the balcony.

Water

Water availability is important. One or more hose bibs, installed on the outside walls of the balcony is ideal. A second alternative is, as required, to attach a small diameter hose to a bathroom or kitchen faucet, passing it through a window to the balcony. Remember that if you have fairly extensive planting, carrying water in watering cans can be a real chore.

Safety

Safety is a major consideration. Is the balcony strong enough to carry the weight of planters, containers, soil and screens etc. as well as the gardeners and their friends? Check with the building manager, and if there is any doubt, consult with an engineer.

Also, in planning, make provision to prevent things from rolling, skidding and dropping off your balcony onto balconies and people below.

Design

Prepare a scale lay-out of the balcony garden indicating the precise location and size of planned planters, containers, window boxes, railing boxes, hanging containers attached to the balcony above— wall brackets and Johnny poles— screens, trellises, furniture and environmental modifications (see The Upstairs Environment).

Be sure to adequately provide for people to move around in the garden, shift furniture and carry out maintenance.

Control of drainage water is important. Keep containers inside peripheral railings and within the balcony. Follow the intended drainage system and pattern for the balcony floor.

To facilitate the design process, use successive overlays of cheap sketching paper. When you have frozen on the final design, draw it to scale on your site plan.

Planters and containers

It is possible to construct permanent planters against the walls of the building, sitting on the floor of the balcony. If this is allowed by your landlord, be sure to protect the walls and floor from water damage by using a layer of heavy gauge vinyl, polyethylene or butyl between the soil mass and the walls and floor. Better still, build the planter with a wooden wall, leaving a small gap between it and the building wall. Other, heavy planters and containers may be built separately and, if made of wood, placed on wooden blocks or bricks, above the floor and slightly away from walls. This will also prevent basal rotting and ensure good drainage.

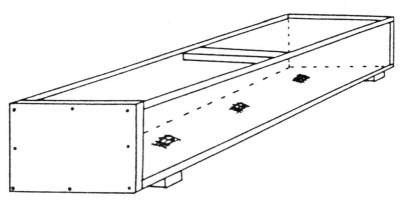

Window Box

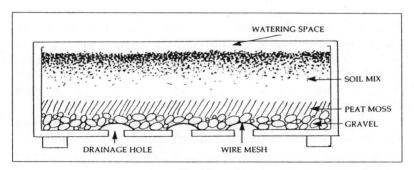

WATERING SPACE

SOIL MIX

PEAT MOSS
GRAVEL

DRAINAGE HOLE   WIRE MESH

Box construction

Most planters and containers will be more or less portable. Heavier kinds may be fitted with castors to facilitate movement and allow for occasional rearrangements. This also allows them to be rolled indoors overnight when early and late frosts threaten, or moved to chase or avoid the sun.

There are a wide variety of manufactured planters available in equally wide ranges of shapes, sizes, materials, qualities and prices. Some of the shapes include bowls, urns, dishes, pots and boxes. Materials include terra-cotta, clay, concrete, stone, plastic and wood.

While it is possible to grow plants in containers of any size, smaller kinds, especially when holding larger plants, frequently dry out. Generally, a minimum size for a container is 20 cm wide and 20 cm deep. An ideal container would be 22.5 to 30 cm deep and any width beyond the 20 cm minimum.

A standard wooden container

A floor-standing, wooden container, particularly suitable for growing vegetables but also good for flowers is easy to construct. Using 200 mm particle board or marine plywood, construct an open-top, rectangular box, 120 cm long, 40 cm wide and 30 cm deep, sitting on two, 5 cm x 10 cm x 40 cm cross-runners. In the bottom, drill a 2 cm drainage hole, every 30 cm line the box with heavy gauge polyethylene, punching holes in it, corresponding with the drainage holes in the bottom of the box. Fix a piece of galvanized mesh over the drainage holes.

Use brass screws for construction. And be sure to steep the boards in a non-toxic, non-petroleum based wood preservative prior to assembly. Finish the outside of the box with a good quality water-proof paint.

The box is now ready for filling which is the subject of the next chapter— soils, manures and fertilizers.

Soils and Nutrition

The general requirements for soils in containers and planters are that they be granular in structure, (comprising discrete, separate particles of various sizes), porous, (containing plenty of air/water spaces between the soil particles), well-drained (surplus water easily exiting the soil in a vertical direction), water retentive and fertile (containing adequate plant foods).

John Innes compost (modified)

A time-honoured, loam-based potting compost, developed in Britain more than forty five years ago, is excellent for the vast majority of plants in containers on balconies where weight is not a problem. It comprises, by bulk:

7 parts medium textured loam top soil,
3 parts granular, sterile, sphagnum peat-moss,
2 parts very coarse, washed sand.

Peat-based Mix

If weight is a problem, or if you have a personal preference, one of the premixed, peat-based potting composts may be used. Of these, the Cornell Type mix is popular and easy to prepare.

Mix together, equal parts of granulated sphagnum peat-moss and #4 grade horticultural vermiculite. To each 2.5 cu. ft. of this mixture, add 10 level tablespoons of ground chalk or limestone, 5 level tablespoons of saltpetre and 1 gallon of warm water.

Perlite may be used where good sand is not obtainable, or if weight is a consideration.

To each 2.5 cu. ft. of this mixture, add 6 ounces of 5-10-5 fertilizer and 3 ounces of ground chalk or limestone.

Be sure that all ingredients are thoroughly mixed together.

Other loam-based composts

In my opinion, the advantages of loam based composts, such as the John Innes, far outweigh any disadvantages.

Since they are loam-based, they are likely to contain most of the essential plant foods including the trace nutrients. Also, like in-ground soils, they are continually producing additional nutrients through weathering, breaking down the mineral components of the soil.

Twenty-five percent of the compost is peat-moss, thereby providing plenty of organic matter which retains lots of soil water while maintaining the soil in a porous condition.

The coarse sand or perlite assure adequate drainage and soil porosity.

The disadvantages are the variability of different kinds of loam and, as far as balconies are concerned, their weight. Although when any compost is thoroughly saturated with water, it's heavy.

Peat-based mixtures

Peat-perlite and peat-vermiculite composts are well-drained, porous, very water-retentive, light weight and easy to prepare.

Over time, they reduce in volume by oxidation of the peat-moss. Plants in them do not form such a stable root anchorage as those in loam-based composts. Since such mixtures contain very little plant foods; and since nutrients are readily leached out of them via drainage waters, plants in them require feeding more often than those in soil-based mixes.. They are fine for annual vegetable and flower crops but not as suitable for trees, shrubs and herbaceous perennials.

The life of a soil mix

In my opinion, the life of a soil-based mix in containers is indeterminate. We have been using the original, John Innes compost to grow annual flowers in twenty five, 22.75 cm deep containers for the past nine years, with excellent results.

Each year, we apply a sprinkling of 13-16-10 fertilizer and thoroughly mix it with the soil. Occasionally, an inch of moist peat-moss is also mixed in. Should the porosity and drainage characteristics of the mix deteriorate, we plan to thoroughly mix in, additional coarse sand or perlite. So far, we have not encountered any soil texture difficulties, nutritional deficiencies or soil-borne pest problems. If we do, the soil can easily be replaced.

Similarly with peat-based mixes, all that's needed is to add fertilizer, top up the containers each year with fresh mix to compensate for any that may have been lost through oxidation, and mix thoroughly.

Plant foods

Plants obtain the foods, hydrogen and oxygen from soil water, via their roots, and carbon (from carbon dioxide) through their leaves. Using the energy of sunlight and the properties of chlorophyll, they manufacture simple sugars from these raw materials. These sugars form a base for the

COMMON INORGANIC FERTILIZER BLENDS OR MIXTURES*

Nitrogen (N)	% nutrient by weight Phosphorous (P)	Potassium (K)	Common uses
8	24	24	flowering plants
8	38	15	root vegetables
13	16	10	all purpose
10	52	10	plant starter
15	30	15	all purpose
20	20	20	all purpose and containers
20	10	5	leafy vegetables
4	12	4	root vegetables
5	10	5	all purpose
25	5	20	leafy vegetables
30	10	10	coniferous evergreens
28	14	14	deciduous trees and shrubs
15	30	10	flowering plants
15	15	30	tomatoes
20	24	14	roses
18	18	24	vegetables and tomatoes
18	18	21	tomatoes
30	10	10	(miracid) acid loving plants
10	14	21	vegetables
10	10	27	(phostrogen) all purpose

* Availability and pH reaction varies (see information on the package).

development of proteins and other, more elaborate, compounds required for growth and reproduction.

All other nutrients are obtained from the soil through the plants root system, including all-important nitrogen, a necessary component of proteins.

Essential plant foods

In addition to hydrogen, oxygen and carbon, there are 16 other essential (soil-borne) nutrients, separated into two classifications— macronutrients and micronutrients. These two terms do not refer to the relative importance of the nutrients but to the relative quantities in which they are used by plants. All are essential!

Macronutrients, required in the largest quantities, include: nitrogen, potassium, calcium, magnesium, phosphorus and sulphur. Required in small or trace amounts are the micronutrients: chlorine, boron, iron, manganese, zinc, copper and molybdenum.

Fortunately, most micronutrients are available in loam-based mixes and seldom need adding to the soil. When required, they can be supplied by special soil or fertilizers.

The four major plant foods

Four of the macronutrients are most often, significantly manipulated by gardeners: nitrogen, phosphorous, potassium and calcium.

Nitrogen (N), as a principle constituent of protein, helps to forge the building blocks of plant growth. It promotes the growth of shoots and leaves and is responsible for the mid to deep-green colour of healthy, vigorous plants.

Phosphorus (P) promotes the development of extensive, vigorous root systems and the size and quality of flowers, fruits and seeds.

Potassium (K), while not used directly by plants, promotes the proper utilization of other plant foods, and early ripening. It is also involved in the development of the mechanical strength of shoots and stems, and resistance to diseases.

Calcium is an important component of the glue (calcium pectate) that sticks plant cells together. However, it has another important role, outside the plant, in the soil. Calcium, or a lack thereof, affects the acidity - alkalinity balance or pH of the soil. Soil acidity can be reduced and therefore, alkalinity increased by the application of calcium, usually in the form of ground limestone or chalk.

Additional manures and composts

Organic matter

From a gardeners point of view, organic matter is anything that was formerly alive. It includes animal manures, garden compost, leaf mould and peat-moss, (forms that, when moist, are in some stage of decomposition): and hoof and horn meal, bone-meal, bone flour and dried blood (forms that are static and dry).

Peat-moss is a unique form of organic matter. While it contains very little plant food, it decomposes very slowly in the soil, thereby exerting a very long- term effect on soil structure. Since it may hold up to ten times its own weight in water, it also has a significant impact on soil water retention

Humus

When organic matter is mixed with a soil, it gradually breaks down to form a dark-brown to blackish coloured, formless substance that thereafter decomposes more slowly, called humus.

Humus improves soil structure, porosity, drainage and fertility by helping to glue sand particles together and by separating the tightly bonded particles of clay. It mixes intimately with clay particles to form clay humus colloids, the seat of much chemical activity in the soil, resulting in the availability of plant foods.

Organic matter and the resultant humus, release the plant foods, of which they are composed, during decomposition in the soil, re-cycling and making them available to other plants. Bulky manures, in particular, contain small proportion of N, P and K which are released into the soil. These materials also act like a sponge, holding water in the soil.

During their breakdown, carbon dioxide is released which combines with water to form weak carbonic acid. This reacts with the mineral components of the soil, releasing available plant foods and enriching the soil.

Most fertile soils contain a population of active, healthy soil organisms including insects, earthworms, protozoa, fungi and bacteria. Their activities improve drainage and achieve the decomposition and distribution of organic matter. But for them to thrive, a soil must contain adequate amounts of organic matter. There is therefore a reciprocal relationship between soil organisms, organic matter and soil fertility.

Uses on balconies

A one inch deep layer of well-rotted, bulky animal manure, garden compost or leaf-mould may be applied annually to the soil surface of planters and containers in early summer, as soon as plants are well established. In the fall or following spring, it can be thoroughly mixed with the soil. Among

COMMON ORGANIC FERTILIZERS DERIVED FROM NATURAL MATERIALS

Name of fertilizer	% nutrient by weight			Absorption Rate
	N	P	K	
activated sewer sludge	5	3	0	medium
blood meal	15	1.3	0.7	medium
blood, dried	12 - 15	3	0	medium-fast
bone meal	2 - 4	11 - 21	0.2	slow
coffee grounds, dried	2	0.4	0.7	medium
fish emulsion	5	2	2	medium-fast
fish meal	10	4	0	slow
guano, bird	12	8	3	medium
hoof and horn meal	12.5	1.8	0	slow
phosphate, rock	0	30 - 32	0	very slow
pig manure*	to 0.6	to 0.4	to 0.52	medium
poultry manure*	to 2	to 1.9	to 1.9	medium-fast
seaweed	1.7	5	5	medium-slow
sheep manure*	to 0.9	to 1	to 1	medium
wood ashes	0	7	7	fast

* When damp - not dry.

permanent plants, fork the mulch as deeply as possible into the soil surface, short of seriously disturbing their roots.

These forms may also be used as all or part of the organic matter content of soil mixes, for example, in the John Innes compost, use one part manure and two parts peat-moss instead of three parts peat-moss. Up to 20 per cent by bulk of the total mix may be used with peat-based mixes.

Fertilizers

There are two broad classes of fertilizer — organic and inorganic (the so called chemical fertilizers). Since plants ingest nutrients in the form of pure chemical ions dissolved in soil water, it makes no difference to them whether the source of food is organic or inorganic.

Strictly speaking, organic fertilizers are derived from animal and vegetable sources, although for reasons which are not too clear, naturally occurring minerals are included, even though they are inorganic.

True organic fertilizers have a four advantages. A slight increase in humus results from their decomposition in the soil. Since they break down more slowly in the soil, the foods derived from them are available to plants over a longer period of time. They do not add other, unnecessary substances to the soil. And many of them add some of the micronutrients or trace elements to the soil.

The Numbers on the Bag

By law, the percentages of nitrogen (N), phosphorous (P) and potassium (K) contained in any fertilizer must be printed on the package, always in the same order. Therefore, 5-10-5 printed on a package means that the fertilizer inside contains 5 per cent nitrogen, 10 per cent phosphorous and 5 per cent potssium. The rest of the fertilizer may be filler, carrier materials, inert materials or other chemical materials that don't have to be disclosed.

COMMON INORGANIC FERTILIZERS
MANUFACTURED FROM CHEMICAL SOURCES

Name of fertilizer	% nutrient by weight			Absorption Rate	pH
	N	P	K		
ammonium sulphate	21	0	0	fast	acid
ammonium nitrate	33	0	0	very fast	acid
calcium nitrate	15	0	0	very fast	alaline
sodium nitrate	16	0	0	very fast	alkaline
urea	45	0	0	very fast	acid
ammonium phosphate sulphate	16	20	0	medium	acid
mono ammonium phosphate	11	48	0	medium	acid
di ammonuim phosphate	21	53	0	medium	acid
superphosphate	0	18-25	0	slow	neutral
treble superphosphate	0	45	0	slow	neutral
potassium phosphate	0	22	28	mid	neutral
potassium chloride	0	0	50	fast	neutral
potassium muriate	0	0	60	fast	neutral
potassium sulphate	0	0	50	fast	neutral
potassium nitrate	13-14	0	44-46	fast	alkaline

Disadvantages include: slow availability of plant foods, inability to deliver sufficient amounts of foods during peak demands, many contain small amounts of plant foods, and high cost.

My inclination during initial soil preparation is to ensure a high level of organic matter and humus in the soil and to use both organic and inorganic fertilizers: organic to ensure a steady, long-term supply of nutrients, and inorganic to ensure immediate availability. The annual addition of organic matter and complete fertilizers will maintain a high level of fertility.

For summer feeding, I prefer complete, soluble, inorganic fertilizers.

Bear in mind that due to continuous, frequent leaching (losing dissolved foods via the drainage water) and the relatively small soil volumes and restricted root systems in containers, there is a need for feeding more frequently with readily available plant foods than with in-ground garden plants (See tables of fertilizers.).

Using fertilizers in containers

In addition to incorporating some organic matter each year, thoroughly mix complete fertilizers with the soil prior to planting. This means fertilizers that contain N, P and K.

Although I never use them, many gardeners recommend the use of very soluble, high phosphorus, plant starter fertilizers to "water in" transplants. Apparently, they get the roots off to a good start and reduce the stress of transplanting. We have found that careful and proper transplanting into well prepared fertile soil, and the correct after-care is enough.

Once annual plants are well-established and growing vigorously in containers and planters, its time to begin regular feeding. Use a water-soluble, complete fertilizer once every 10 to 15 days throughout the balance of the growing season. The actual frequency will depend on your observation of the general vigour, foliage colour, rate of shoot and leaf development, and in the case of flowers, the quantity, size and quality of the blooms.

If you are a patient gardener who has the time, feeding at half the recommended rate and twice the frequency is a good strategy for encouraging uniform plant growth.

General
Gardening Operations

In addition to soil preparation, the successful balcony gardener needs to master a few basic gardening operations and techniques.

Filling the containers

With containers and planters that sit on runners, blocks, bricks or other objects designed to keep them off the balcony floor, be sure they have adequate drainage holes in their bases. For bottomless planters and solid based kinds that sit directly on the floor, be sure that drainage holes are in the base of their side boards at or near ground level.

Fix over each drainage hole, a piece of 4 mm galvanized wire mesh to prevent soil from running out.

For individual containers to 45 cm long and wide and to 30 cm deep, including window boxes, no other drainage is necessary.

For containers and planters with and without bottoms, larger than 45 cm long and wide, and 30 or more cm deep, place a 3 cm deep layer of 1.75 cm washed gravel, covered by a 2.5 cm deep layer of coarse peat-moss or a piece of landscape construction fabric over the base.

Fill the container with soil mix, in 10 cm layers, thoroughly firming each with the fingers. For containers, 30 cm or more across and long leave the soil level 2.5 cm below the rim to facilitate proper watering. 2.0 cm is adequate for containers, 20 to 30 cm across.

After filling, water thoroughly to settle and saturate the soil.

Seed sowing

Station sowing

Since very small quantities of seed are involved in growing annual vegetables and flowers in balcony gardens by direct outdoor seeding, in many cases, it will be most practical to sow in stations. This is the practice of deciding exactly where you wish each plant to grow, then placing three seeds by hand at each location.

Using a small rake or a hand-fork, rake over a patch of soil at each station to produce a seed-bed of fine soil about an inch deep. Alternatively, especially if you are planning to seed the whole planter at once, prepare the entire soil surface of the planter. Place three seeds at each station, pushing them gently into the soil to the correct depth and cover with fine soil. If you have the patience and desire the best results, cover the seeds with moist peat-moss, vermiculite or perlite. "Water in" gently with a fine sprinkle. Place a stake or label at each station for later identification and keep a record of what is sown.

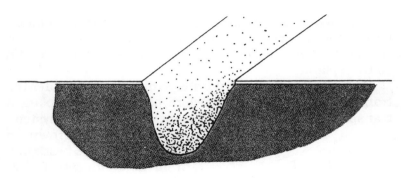

Seed Drill

Subsequently water lightly, little and often, until sprouting occurs. Be sure to avoid puddling the soil surface and washing out the seed when watering. When the seedlings have sprouted, thin them out by nipping the weakest with your thumb nail or kitchen scissors, leaving only the strongest at each station to grow and mature.

Row sowing

Quick maturing, smaller vegetables such as baby carrots, scallions and radishes, that are not normally thinned out, may be sown to mature in rows.

After preparing a seed bed, use a blunt pointed stick or stake to make a shallow, more or less "V"-shaped seed drill in the soil surface. A yard-stick will help to keep you on a straight track. Sow the seeds sparsely along the bottom of the drill and cover them. "Water in" as previously described. After germination, allow them to grow and mature without disturbance.

Planting transplant seedlings

Many annual flowers and several vegetables are grown from transplant seedlings (transplants). These are plants, originally sown in a greenhouse and "pricked out" or transplanted at regular intervals into shallow trays where they are "grown on" for sale.

Cabbage, Brussels sprouts, cauliflowers and other members of the cabbage family may be grown in cold frames or cool greenhouses in rows. The bare-root seedlings are sold as transplants.

Regardless of the type of transplant, be sure to water the transplants, several hours before planting. Never plant a transplant, seedling or potted plant with a dry root system.

Cold frame

With plants grown in plastic trays, the best kind, from the standpoint of minimal planting disturbance, are in individual cells. These are simply removed from the cells without much damage to their root systems and planted out.

Those grown in a single, undivided plastic tray need to be separated. Use a sharp knife to cut between the plants, leaving each plant in an equal size, rectangular block of soil.

In both cases, roots poking through the holes in the bottom of the tray, may be first, cut off.

Using a garden trowel, make a hole at the planting location, deep and wide enough to accommodate the root-soil ball. Place the root-soil ball in the hole and by pushing the trowel into the soil to the sides of the plant and slightly levering it towards the root-soil ball, bring the soil into intimate contact with the root-soil ball. The top of the root-soil ball should be no more than 2 cm below finished soil level.

Members of the cabbage family may be planted with a trowel or a dibber (a short piece of broom handle with a blunt tapered end). The finished soil level should be about 2.5 cm above the top-most roots.

Planting from plant-bands and pots

Tomatoes, cucumbers, bell peppers, eggplants, geraniums (Pelargoniums), fuchsias and other plants may be grown in pots. The tricky part is knocking the plant out of its pot. Lay your hand over the soil surface with the plant stem between your third and fourth fingers. Turn the pot upside-down. Holding the pot with your spare hand, sharply rap its rim on the edge of an outdoor table, bench or chair etc. Alternatively use a trowel handle to tap upwards on the rim. In the first case the soil ball will drop down and in the second the pot will lift up. In either case you should be left with the ball sitting on your hand. Using a trowel, simply make a hole wide and deep enough to accommodate the root-soil ball and plant as previously described.

Unless bottomless, plant bands are best carefully removed, causing as little disturbance to the roots as possible, prior to planting. It depends on the integrity of the root-soil ball. If it looks dicey, cut out the bottom of the band and cut its rim down to soil level. Plant as previously described

Planting plants grown in peat or soil blocks is very straightforward.

Watering

Due to the relatively small volumes and shallow soils in containers and planters, the extensive root systems developed by plants in such restricted conditions, the foliage canopies covering soil areas and shedding rain onto the balcony floor, the relatively fast drainage of container soils, and the balcony environment, plants in containers tend to dry out more frequently and more extensively than those, in-ground.

Bear in mind that environmental factors that increase a need for water include heat, direct sunlight, wind and low humidity.

The general rule of watering, except for seeds, is to water copiously when needed but leave as long an interval as possible between waterings. This helps to develop deep, drought resistant root systems. The rule applies to plants on balconies until they are well established. Then its a matter of close, regular observation; although copious watering is still required.

Depending on weather conditions and the size of a container, well established plants, especially later in the season, may require watering every day or two. In extreme conditions, smaller containers may need watering twice daily.Trickle irrigation and wick watering systems can be used.

Feeding and mulching

Before feeding, be sure the soil is moist. Don't feed plants in dry soil. Mix and apply the fertilizer exactly in accordance with the manufacturer's directions. Do not apply stronger than recommended. A Haws-type watering can is a real asset. Otherwise use a watering can with a fine "rose"— that's the round thing with holes in it that fits on the spout. Beware of eroding holes in the soil when feeding and watering.

Weeding and aerating

In a balcony garden, since soil surface areas are minimal, weeding is easiest done by hand pulling. Weeding is much easier when the soil is moist, so plan your weeding a day after rain or watering. Get a good grip on the weed in question and using a firm but gentle, continuous, upward pull, remove it from the soil. For larger weeds or those fixed very firmly in the soil, use a small stick or plant label to loosen the soil around the base of the weed and act as a lever before pulling. The best and easiest time to weed is when they are in the small seedling stage.

Light and shallow forking-over and stirring the soil surface about 2 cm deep will loosen soil surface compaction, admit air into the soil and allow trapped carbon dioxide and other unneeded gases to escape into the atmosphere. A shallow layer of fine soil particles at soil level will also help to conserve soil water by acting as an insulating dust mulch and prevent the germination and establishment of weeds.

This practice is only needed until a summer mulch of organic matter has been applied to the soil surface, or has not been used.

Such soil cultivation may be carried out using a hand fork, small cultivator or hand hoe.

Staking

Some of the weaker-stemmed and/or taller-growing plants may require supporting with stakes or proprietary wire support systems.

Stakes are available in a wide range of materials, thicknesses and lengths — old-fashioned bamboo and modern plastics being among the favourites. Stakes should be coloured green to be unobtrusive in use.

Be sure to select a stake long and thick enough to do the job at hand.

Place the stake behind the plant so it is hidden by the plant stem and foliage. Push it vertically into the soil, 2-4 cm away from the stem, deep enough to provide support to the growing plant.

To tie, stand behind the stake. Using, moistened raffia, garden twine, wire twisters or, preferably a flat plastic tying

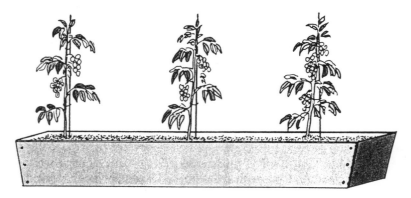

Staked cherry tomatoes

tape, make a complete loop round the stake, then loop the tying material round the plant stem, finally tying the knot against the stake. This method avoids bruising or crushing the stem, prevents slippage of the tie down the stake, and is easier to do.

Another method of support is by using several stakes placed equidistantly around the perimeter or within the body of a plant or group of plants. Tying material is then strung, criss-cross between stakes, forming a network through which the plants can grow.

Dead-heading

Dead-heading is the practice of cutting off flower-heads, plus a piece of the stem below, back to a non-flowered shoot or bud. This encourages the production of more flowers and shoots from the lower reaches of the plants.

Continually pick off and dispose of dead, yellowed and diseased leaves. Keep current with weeding.

Growing Flowers

In this chapter, specific uses and methods of cultivation are discussed. For soil preparation and general methods of cultivation, please refer to Chapters 2 and 3 as appropriate.

Annuals and herbaceous perennials

Due to the relatively small amount of space available for planting in most balcony gardens; and since most herbaceous perennials only flower over a short period and require quite a bit of space; and since the prudent balcony gardener will wish to put flower-gardening efforts where they result in an optimum yield — in a balcony garden, it makes good sense to concentrate on growing annuals and those plants which are treated as such.

Annuals

Annuals grow from seed, flower, set seed and die in a single growing season. Some tender perennials, bulbs, tubers and corms are treated as annuals. These include: geranium (pelargonium), fuchsia, begonia, gladiolus, canna, dahlia, snapdragon and gazania.

Most annuals are of low, often compact, stature (not requiring staking and tying), leafy (covering bare soil and crowding-out weeds), very floriferous, over a three to four month period, and easy to grow.

Annuals are well-adapted to life in containers of all shapes and sizes, including the traditional window, railing and fence-top boxes.

Biennials

Biennials grow from seed, pass their first growing season in an above-ground, vegetative, non-flowering state, then flower, set seed and die during the second growing season. In their flowering year, many biennials have a relatively short flowering period.

Perennials

Perennials grow from seed. Most do not flower until the second, and in some cases the third, growing season. They are also raised from plant divisions and cuttings, flowering sooner.

Generally, once established, they live three or more years. They produce new foliage and flowering shoots each year, arising at or near ground level. In the fall they naturally die down to near or below ground level, leaving dormant underground bulbs, corms, tubers, tuberous roots buds or shootlets, or near ground- level shootlets.

Many perennials are too large, too leafy and too vigorous (demanding more root-run and soil depth than most containers can provide) for balcony gardens — although there are some, particularly those with attractive foliage, dwarf habit and longer flowering periods that may be worthy of trial, especially in larger containers, either alone or mixed with annuals.

Other disadvantages, especially with larger and more vigorous kinds includes the need for staking and tying, and outgrowing their allotted space and/or entire container.

Arranging flowering plants

When selecting and arranging plants in balcony gardens, bear in mind that space is limited. Unless your inclinations are those of the botanical collector (and there's nothing wrong with such inclinations if that's your bent), it will probably be prudent to be rather selective and restrictive in your choice of plants.

It is not possible to grow the wide array of plants that may be accommodated in the average urban garden. To attempt a too ambitious variety of plants can only lead to uncoordinated "bitty and busy" arrangements that offend the senses.

Height

Be sure to know the height that your choices will achieve by the end of the growing season or at their peak of development. This knowledge will allow you to place plants in both graded-slope and less geometric arrangements.

Generally, tall plants should be placed at the rear of containers backing against a wall; at the shady ends and sides of containers to prevent shading other plants; and in the centre of containers that are sunny and evenly illuminated.

From a design point of view, tall plants provide interesting form. They may be used to contrast with rounded and low forms.

Form

Plants exhibit various forms which can be exploited by the gardener. Some are upright, rounded or low-spreading while others are trailing or climbing. Forms may be used to create interest, harmony and contrast in a planting.

Texture

Texture is best explained by describing its two poles - coarse and fine. Coarse textured plants have large, distinct leaves, borne more or less sparsely on stout stems. On the other hand, those with fine texture have very small leaves, rather densely borne on slender stems.

Foliage colour also has an influence on texture. Dark greens tend to reinforce the idea of coarse texture, whereas pale greens and greys appear more fine textured.

There are many gradations of texture between these two poles.

Again texture may be used in the design of planting arrangements.

Colour

A very important design consideration, plant colour is manifest in two ways — foliage colour and flower colour.

The most common foliage colours are reddish-purples, purples, yellows, silvers and variegated with white or yellow.

A major benefit of foliage colour is its long term — all season long — from planting to killing frost.

With annuals, the season of floral colour comes a close second, with plants like geraniums (pelargoniums) and fuchsias, rivalling foliage colour. Masses of solid colour are more effective than mixed colours or spotty arrangements. Bear in mind that very bright, intense colours may produce a high glare in bright sunshine. Use more subdued colours in full sun and save the brightest for the shadier places. However, bear in mind that white and yellow, although bright colours, are not a their best in the shade.

Colours opposite each other are said to be complementary. Those adjacent to each other are called, analogous. Both complementary and analogous colours can be planted together to produce harmonious combinations.

The basic or primary colours are red, blue and green. The addition of white to these and their derivatives, results in different "tints". Different "shades" result from the addition of black. And the addition of grey, results in different "tones".

As white, black or grey are added to pure colours, they decrease in strength or purity. This is called a decrease in "chroma"

Here are a few suggested combinations based on the Birren System for Outdoor Colour:

Blue may be used with: scarlet and buff; white and yellow; orange and scarlet; other chromas of blue; and yellow or orange of the same chroma as the blue in question.

Violet, purple and magenta are colours between the primary colours of blue and red.

Hues closer to blue may be used together or with tints and shades of blue.

Hues closer to red may be used with tints or shades of red.

Violet or purple are effective when used with yellow or yellow-green foliage. They may also be used for contrasting with yellow and white flowers.

Red and scarlet are excellent with dense, green foliage.
Use to harmonize with red-violet and red-orange hues.
Use with white or a clear blue for contrast.

Pink will appear more intense when used with white.
Pinks blend well with other colours of similar chroma.

Orange goes well with reds, browns, bronzes, turquoise-blue, creamy-white or yellow. Purple flowers and bright green foliage is an excellent complement.

Yellow looks good with blues of equal chroma, and white.

White softens low colours when mixed with them, and strengthens high value colours.

Grey and silver are used to lighten masses of dark green, add an illusion of distance, and to mediate among otherwise conflicting colours.
Avoid dotting them among bright colours but do use in masses.

Sowing annuals directly outdoors

While the more traditional method of growing annuals is from transplants, it is practical to sow several kinds directly outdoors at the sites where they are to flower.

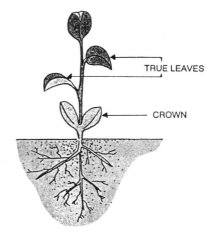

A seedling showing its true leaves.

Timing

The hardiest annuals may be sown, depending on local climatic conditions, in April and early May. The more

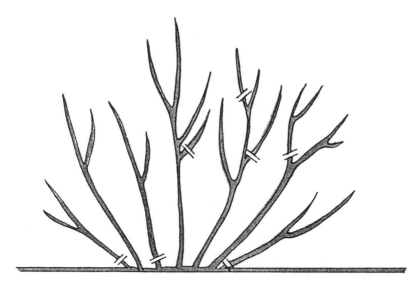

Pruning a transplant.

tender, half hardy kinds are not sown until the minimum soil temperature at night reaches 12°C and danger of frost during germination is passed.

Sowing

The best method is station sowing, thinning out to one strong healthy seedling per station.

Transplanting annuals

Transplants are usually grown in greenhouses and cold-frames in flats or trays, pots and plant bands. The best kinds of trays are divided into small individual root cells. Plants from these, suffer minimal stress when transplanted. Plants in pots and bands also suffer less stress.

Good quality plants exhibit non-woody, compact growth (short jointed), mid to dark green, unblemished leaves, signs of recent vigorous growth of stems and leaves, and (although not an essential sign of good development) a few flower buds and an occasional flower. Woody plants in full flower may be a sign that they are overly root-bound and starved.

Avoid plants that are leggy, woody (excepting geraniums, fuchsias and other shrubby plants), pale green or yellowish which lack vigour and are in full flower.

Extending the season

Since early fall frost is often followed by an open, sunny, frost-free period, it is worthwhile protecting annuals from its first nip. We should do all possible to extend the seasonal life of the balcony garden. Its a small enough garden that can be kept going for a small enough expenditure of effort and cash.

Containers on castors may be moved indoors for a few nights. Smaller containers and hanging pots may also be easily moved indoors.

Moving containers and window boxes close to the building walls will provide a slight measure of protection from radiant heat. This can be intensified by covering plants with a few layers of newspaper, heavy brown wrapping paper, or burlap, held above the plants on a lightweight temporary frame. Agricultural Fleece is a lightweight insulating material that can be laid directly on the plants.

The entire balcony can be enclosed using heavy polyethylene. The inside temperature can be increased by leaving the balcony door open overnight.

If your balcony garden is permanent, consider building one or more cold-frames to protect your containers for a few nights. These can be knock-down, portable, easily stored units. Make them with a plywood front, back and sides and a lightweight top cover made of 5 X 5 cm lumber. Cover inside and out with an 8 mil. polyethylene film, i.e. leaving a 5 cm air space between. If you wish to be sophisticated, a small heater-fan may be placed inside the frame.

The disadvantages of cold frames are that they have to be stored when not in use, and take up extra room on the balcony when being used— although this may not be so bad if taken into account when planning the garden.

Fall clean-up

After the frosts finally kill the plants or they have definitely finished blooming for the year, pull-up the plants and dispose of them. Don't be afraid to leave old roots in the soil. They will eventually decompose, adding to the organic matter.

Depending on the depth of soil in the container, use a border or hand fork to turn over the soil to its full depth, roughly mixing in any residual, summer mulch. Leave the soil in large clods to expose as much soil surface area as possible to the beneficial weathering and cleansing effects of snow, rain, freeze and thaw.

Growing Herbaceous Perennials

Planting

Planting root clumps or container-grown plants is the best all-round practice leading to quick establishment and significant results. Dig the planting hole deep and wide enough to accommodate the roots or root-soil ball. Do not cover any deeper than one-half inch above the existing soil level on the root-soil ball. Place and firm the soil around the roots. Water, immediately following planting.

Thinning Shoots

Some herbaceous perennials that produce an abundance of closely spaced shoots may be thinned out to 4 to 8 widely and evenly spaced shoots (depending on vigour) to encourage the production of fewer but taller, stronger shoots, bearing larger flowers of higher quality.

This should be done early in the year, as soon as the shoots are readily identified and large enough to handle. Using a sideways, levering motion, break off the weakest, most over-crowded shoots, below or at ground level. Tougher shoots may be nipped off with the thumbnail or cut, using scissors.

Fall Clean-up

In late fall, cut back all flowered shoots, and leaves that normally die down to ground level, to ground level. Leave at or just above ground level the foliage of those kinds that do not naturally die back below ground level.

Using a hand-fork, loosen the soil between plants to a reasonably fine texture, leaving a level surface.

Growing Vegetables

Most vegetables are easy to grow in containers, provided they are deep enough, and there is sufficient light on the balcony.

Suitable containers

Tomatoes, cucumbers, zucchini, bush type squash, egg-plant and bell-peppers are often best when grown alone in separate containers, approximately 22.5 cm deep and 30 cm wide.

The light environment

Ideally, most vegetables should be exposed to 8 hours of direct sun per day at mid-summer, although good crops may be obtained with 6 hours per day. Shelter from winds is essential.

CONTAINERS FOR GROWING VEGETABLES
APPROXIMATE MINIMUM SIZE

Vegetable	# plants/ container	width (cm)	depth (cm)	Patio varieties
beans - bush	3	20	20 to 25	no
beans - pole- staked	1	30	20	no
beets	several	20+	15 to 30	yes
broccoli	1	30	30	no
brussels sprouts	1	30	30	no
cauliflower	1	30	30	no
cabbage	1	20 to 25	30	no
carrots	several	20+	25 to 30	yes
corn	3	50	20	yes
cucumbers	1	20	30	yes
eggplant	1	30	30	yes
endive	1	15	15	no
kale	1	20	20	no
lettuce - head	1	20	20	yes
lettuce - leaf	2	20	20	no
mustard	1	20	20	no
onions	several	20+	15	no
garlic	several	20+	15	no
peas - staked	several	20+	yes	
peppers	1	30	30	yes
radish	several	20+	15	no
spinich	1	20	15	no
squash - bush	1	60	60	yes
squash - vine - staked	1	60	60	no
swiss chard	1	20	20	no
turnips	1	15	20	no
tomato - dwarf - staked	1	30	60	yes
tomato - bush	1	25	30	no
tomato - staked	1	30	30	no

Tomatoes, cucumbers, egg-plant, bell-peppers and melons prefer the sunniest and warmest possible locations, followed by bush, snap, French, pole and Lima beans, and corn.

Beets, broad-beans, broccoli, brussels sprouts, cabbage, Chinese cabbage, cauliflower, other cole or Brassica crops, celery, celeriac, garlic, leek, onion, lettuce, parsley, parsnip, radish, turnip, carrot, rutabaga, peas, potatoes, spinach and Swiss chard all appreciate reasonably sunny but cool growing conditions.

Shade tolerant kinds

Of the cool season crops, peas, carrots, bunching onions or scallions, lettuce, spinach and Chinese cabbage are the most shade tolerant kinds.

Those kinds worth a try in semi-shaded spots include endive, kale, mustard greens, radish, turnip, Swiss chard, chives, mint and parsley.

Selection of varieties

Always select those varieties suitable for the local climatic conditions that will mature within the growing season of the region. Sources of information include seed suppliers, reputable garden centres, university and governmental horticultural departments, local horticultural associations and local gardeners.

Succession crops

These are quick-maturing crops, sown or planted in the same plot immediately following the harvest of a previous crop. Depending on the length of the local growing season and the time left for growing a succession crop, suitable kinds include leaf lettuce, spinach, radishes, baby or bunching carrots, beets and turnips, bunching onions, and dwarf peas.

Successional sowing

This is a technique for avoiding gluts. Instead of making one sowing, maturing all at once, several sowings of smaller quantities are sown at 7 to 10 day intervals. In this way a series of smaller crops mature at different times over a longer period. Due to restricted space, this idea may be of limited value in a balcony garden.

Catch crops

Like succession crops, these are quick maturing vegetables sown between slower growing kinds to catch a quick crop before the slower-growing main crop takes up the room and closes its canopy.

Use the same kinds as for succession crops.

Pests and Diseases

Pests

Pests can wreak havoc on a balcony garden if ignored. Careful gardeners will take the same precautions for their balcony garden as they do for their regular gardens. There are several common sense tips you can follow to help your balcony plants fend off unwelcome intruders — in fact, these maintenance ideas can help in any garden.

- Make sure that you keep your garden well-weeded. Some pests can use weeds as hosts or launching points for assaults on your plants. Although weeds are less common in containers than in open garden soil, they can be accidentally be transplanted when you move plants into their containers.

- Always inspect plants for signs of pest eggs, caterpillars and other insects. If you plant with these signs of infestation present, pests will quickly spread to other areas of your balcony garden.

- Keep your garden clean. Remove waste paper, old cuttings and other garden garbage to deny pests an other place to breed and grow.

- Don't grow the same vegetables or flowers in the same container each year. By rotating a variety of plants, you can help prevent any particular pest from gaining a permanent foothold in any given container.

- Make sure you keep all the tools you use in your garden clean and in good shape.

If you already have an infestation, the above guidelines will help your garden recover. A number of chemical insecticides on the market can help you combat these pests. There are also an number of environmentally friendly ways to rid your garden of pests. For more information on chemical insecticides, consult your local gardening centre.

Aphids

These small, soft bodied insects draw sap from the leaves of plants, causing abnormal growth and some discolouration. They will attack most types of plant life. They tend to live in colonies in a variety of cruciferous (cabbage, radishes, etc.) plants. Adult aphids have wings, while nymphs do not. Most aphids are pale-green, but some species are pink, yellow, black or brown.

Aphid

If you spot aphids on your plants, try to remove the colonies as soon as possible. There are chemical insecticides on the market that will remove aphids if you can't dislodge them yourself.

Cruciferous flea beetles

Flea beetles chew small holes in the leaf surface of some vegetables, eventually causing discolouration and leaf death. There favourite targets are cabbage, radishes, turnips and other cruciferous plants. They are especially dangerous to young plants and seedlings, which can be killed if a flea beetle infestation is not stopped quickly. Adults are black or black and yellow and move around by jumping, like fleas. The larvae look like small, white worms and feed on the roots of plants.

To help prevent a flea beetle infestation, make sure you keep your gardening area clear of garbage. Also, make sure your plants are well watered so they can outgrow an infestation. If you suspect that your plants have flea beetles, there are chemical insecticides that can help kill these pests.

Imported cabbage worm, diamondback moth

Both of these caterpillars attack the leaves of cabbages, radishes, turnips and other cruciferous plants. They chew holes through the leaves and can dig into the edible portions of these vegetables. Cabbage worms are green in colour and are about three centimetres in length. Diamondback moth caterpillars are smaller and are pale green in colour.

If you spot these pests on your plants, attempt to remove them by hand. If you don't think you can get them all, there are chemical insecticides that will kill both of these types of caterpillars.

Slugs

Slugs destroy plant foliage by cutting holes in leaves and they can attack most vegetables in your garden. They usually feed at night and thrive in humid, damp conditions. Slugs are greyish-brown, soft-bodied and about 4 centimetres long.

Since this pest thrives in damp, humid places, its a good idea to keep the areas surrounding your balcony or container garden dry. Make sure you get rid of all your gardening garbage, since slugs like to lay their eggs in dark, well hidden places. If you think your garden has a slug problem, you can try to trap them by leaving a saucer of beer near potential hiding places. There are also a number of chemical insecticides on the market that will combat slugs.

Thrips

Thrips rasp the leaves of vegetables and feed on the fluids contained within the leaves. A sign of thrip infestation is white or silvery blotches on leaves. Eventually these leaves turn brown and die. The flowers of some vegetable plants can also be attacked. There are also a number of thrip species which feed on particular

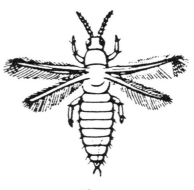

Thrips

vegetables — onion, cabbage, peas and beans to name a few.

There are several chemical insecticides that can destroy thrips.

Leafhoppers

These pests feed on the undersides of leaves of annuals and perennials, producing white spots which eventually turn brown before the leaves die. As the leaves die, the plant itself becomes less healthy and more prone to other pests and diseases. Leafhoppers are green, yellow or white; wedge-shaped and about 1 cm long. They often hop rather than fly.

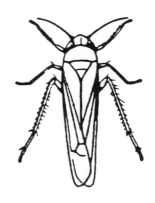

Leafhopper

There are several chemical insecticides that can be used to control leafhoppers.

Spider mites

These tiny insects draw the sap from the leaves of herbaceous ornamentals . Leaves attacked by spider mites exhibit a yellowish stripping where the mites have drained the plant's fluids. Eventually, these strips turn to brown blotches and the leaves die. The plant is weakened — new leaves are buds are deformed.

Spider mites are difficult to see. If you look closely, they look like reddish-yellow or green specs on the underside of leaves. They are accompanied by a fine web-like material, which makes the leaves look dusty.

Chemical insecticides can help take care of spider mite problems.

Whiteflies

Whiteflies also draw fluids from annuals and perennials to survive. Leaves on an infested plant will yellow and die. These pests also leave a sticky, honeydew residue on the leaves, upon which black fungus grows. Adult whiteflies are coated in a white, powder wax. They resemble tiny moths when they're in flight. Nymphs look like flat, oval spots on the undersides of leaves.

Whitefly

Chemical insecticides can be used against whiteflies.

Diseases

Blossom end rot

The first sign of this disease common to peppers and tomatoes is the appearance of a small, water-soaked area at the bottom of the fruit. This area eventually expands and turns dark, hard and leathery on tomatoes or light-coloured and papery on peppers.

The problem is most often an irregular water supply to the fruit. Blossom end rot might also indicate an imbalance in the nutrients supplied to the plant — proportionally too much nitrogen or too little calcium.

To combat this disease make sure that your containers are properly drained to permit an even, regular flow of water through the soil. Stay away from high-nitrogen fertilizers.

Clubroot

This disease can affect vegetables which, at first, seem healthy. The first sign of trouble will be a noticable stunting of the plant's growth. An inspection of the roots will show abnormal, club-shaped nodes swelling out from the roots. This disease can be fatal to the plant if left unchecked. It preys mostly on broccoli, brussels sprouts, cabbage, cauliflower and rutabagas.

Clubroot is caused by a fungus that resides in soil and it is transferred to the roots of a vegetable planted in that soil. Winter won't kill the clubroot fungus, and once soil is infected, it is difficult to remove the fungus.

If you suspect that your containers are infected, it's best to dispose of the infected soil and begin with fresh soil next year.

Leaf spots and blights

In small quantities, leaf spots don't really cause much of a problem. But if the spots become dominant, or if leaf blight (the general and rapid killing of leaves, stems and flowers) sets in, some chemical treatment may be necessary. Leaf spots often are accompanied by a powdery, white growth around the spot.

Leaf spots and blights are caused by a variety of bacteria and fungi. Make sure that you keep your containers free of weeds. If you think there is a problem, apply a commercial fungicide designed for the type of vegetable you are growing.

Rots

Rot refers to the discolouration, softening and eventual destruction of plant tissue. Many of the bacteria and fungi that cause leaf spots and blights also cause rots. It can be combated the same way as you combat leaf spots and blights.

Storage problems

Once your vegetables are picked, they lose the vital lifeline which connects them with the rest of the plant. The are especially susceptible to a variety of diseases at this stage. Vegetables in storage can rot or can turn into a breeding ground for all sorts of fungi.

Here are some things to remember when you store freshly picked vegetables:

- keep the work area, storage area and the vegetables dry. Moist, humid conditions are ideal for a variety of vegetable diseases.

- harvest in the late fall, if possible, when the soil is cooler.

- don't harvest in wet weather.

- try not to bruise or scratch the vegetables while you're harvesting them.

- before you store the vegetables, dry them in a cool, dark place.

- make sure that your storage area is thoroughly cleaned, disinfected and properly ventilated.

Viruses

Often, the only sign that a plant has a virus is a prolonged stunting of growth. Other, rarer, symptoms include ringspots, mosaics, tumors and distortion of the stems and leaves.

To help prevent viruses from attacking your vegetables, try to plant seeds that have been pre-treated to prevent viruses. Maintain a clean gardening area and try to control insects, as they often are responsible for the spread of harmful plant viruses.

White rot

This is a disease which attacks the roots of onions, garlic, leeks and shallots. The first visible symptom is the yellowing of the leaves near the base of the stem. By the time these leaves die, white rot has likely destroyed the plant's root system. If you pull the plant, you will find a number of 1-cm-diameter, black growths throughout the infected parts.

The white rot fungus can survive for many years in soil. It can be transmitted through transplants and by improperly cleaned gardening tools.

To discourage white rot, try to keep your gardening area clean and be sure to properly wash your gardening tools after use. Try rotating your vegetable crops yearly from container to container. If you suspect white rot, consider removing the contaminated soil from the container and replacing it with new soil.

Wilts

If your plants are inexplicably drooping — from stems to leaves to flowers — you may have a case of wilts. Wilts are usually caused by lack of water. Often, bacterial or fungal infections cut off the water supply to various parts of the plant, causing them to wilt.

A seed-protecting fungicide might help if you are experiencing a lot of wilts. Cultivating when the soil is dry and correct fertilization will also deter the spread of wilt-causing infection. You might also try rotating your crops yearly.

Botrytis

If your growing peonies, and the stems suddenly begin to break down and the buds shrivel and blacken, you may have an outbreak of botrytis on your hands. This fungus will destroy newly opening flowers and, in damp conditions, may cause a brown layer of spores to form over the diseased parts.

If you suspect botrytis, immediately destroy the diseased plant parts. Don't plant your peonies too close together and avoid overhead watering.

Powdery mildew

The first signs of powdery mildew are small raised growths on young leaves that are soon covered with a whitish mould. The fungus then continues on to the stems, buds and flowers. Other symptoms include: stunting of growth, discolouration and general growth decline.

Fungicides applied during the first stages of this infection can be effective. Powdery mildew is more likely to strike in shady areas of your balcony, so try planting mildew-resistant flowers in these shady areas. Make sure you give your plants enough room for air circulation.

When to Plant

Now that you've established a plan for your balcony garden and have chosen the types of plants you wish to grow in it, it's time to find out when your plants must be started in order to maximize their growth during gardening season.

The chart on the next two pages will serve as a handy guide on when to get vegetables started..

SEEDING DIRECTLY OUTDOORS OR GROWING FROM TRANSPLANTS

	Sowing Date (wks)*	Depth (cm)	Spacing (cm)	Successional Sowing (wks)	Last Sowing**	Indoor Seeding (wks)*	Planting (wks)*	Maximum Age (wks)***	Seed to Harvest
asparagus	—3 to 4	3 to 4	45	no	no	10 to 18	—3 to + 4	12 to 14	3 years
beans - snap	0	4 to 5	15	1 to 2	8	3	+ 1-2	3 to 4	6 to 8
beans - broad	—5 to 7	4 to 5	20	no	no	no	no	no	12 to 13
beets	—3 to 4	1 to 2.5	15	2 to 3	8	8	—4	4	7 to 8
broccoli	—3 to 4	0.5 to 1.5	45	2 to 3	11 to 12	6 to 12	—4	6 to 8	8 to 10
brussels sprouts	—4 to 6	0.5 to 1.5	45	no	no	6 to 12	—4	6 to 8	12 to 16
cabbage - early	—3 to 4	0.5 to 1.5	30 to 40	3 to 4	10	6 to 11	+ 2-3	6 to 8	9 to 10
cabbage - mid-season	—2 to 3	0.5 to 1.5	30 to 40	3 to 4	10	5 to 8	+ 2-3	6 to 8	11 to 13
cabbage - late	0	0.5 to 1.5	30 to 40	no	no	4 to 6	+ 2-3	6 to 8	10 to 16
carrots	5 to 7	0.5 to 1.5	7 to 8	2 to 3	9 to 10	9 to 10	—4	5 to 6	8 to 13
cauliflower	0	0.5 to 1.5	45	2 to 3	9 to 10	6 to 12	—4	6 to 8	8 to 16
celery	1 to 2	0.3 to 0.5	20 to 25	no	no	5 to 7	+ 1-2	6 to 8	13 to 20
cucumber	+1	2 to 5	45	2 to 3	7 to 9	4 to 5	—1P to + 2	2 to 3	7 to 9
eggplant	0	1.5 to 2	60	no	no	10	+ 2-3	8 to 10	8 to 12
endive	—2 to 1	0.5 to 1.5	20	no	no	4 to 8	—4 to + 2	4 to 5	11 to 14
garlic (cloves)	—4 to 6	2.5	15	no	no	8 to 10	—24 to + 1	4 to 6	13 to 16
kale	4 to 6	0.5 to 1.5	45	no	no	6 to 11	—5 to + 2	6 to 8	7 to 9
kohl rabi	4 to 6	0.5 to 1.5	20 to 25	2	4	6 to 11	—5 to + 2	6 to 8	9 to 10
leek	1 to 2	1.5 to 2	15	no	no	10	—5 to + 2	4 to 8	12 to 21
lettuce - iceberg	—4 to 5	0.5 to 1	30	no	no	6 to 12	—6 to + 3	4 to 6	10 to 14
lettuce - romaine	—4 to 5	0.5 to 1	20 to 25	2 to 3	11	6 to 12	—6 to + 3	4 to 6	10 to 14
lettuce - leaf	—5 to 7	0.5 to 1	25	2 to 3	7	5 to 8	—2-3 to + 3	3 to 5	6 to 7

	Sowing Date (wks)*	Depth (cm)	Spacing (cm)	Successional Sowing (wks)	Last Sowing**	Indoor Seeding (wks)*	Planting (wks)*	Maximum Age (wks)***	Seed to Harvest
melon - canteloupe	+1 to 2	1.5 to 2.5	45	no	no	4 to 5	+2	5	15 to 19
onions	−5 to 7	1 to 2	15	no	no	10	−5-7 to +2	4 to 6	13 to 25
parsnip	−2 to 4	0.5 to 1	15	no	no	8 to 10	−4 to + 3-4	4 to 6	11 to 17
peas - early	−5 to 7	2.5 to 5	15	2 to 3	9 to 10	8	−4 to + 2-3	4	8 to 11
peas - mid-season	−5 to 7	2.5 to 5	15	2 to 3	10	8	−4 to + 2-3	4	8 to 11
peas - late	−5 to 7	2.5 to 5	15	2 to 3	11	8	−4 to + 2-3	4	8 to 11
peppers - sweet	−1	0.5 to 1	35 to 40	no	no	10	+2-3	6 to 8	9 to 10
peppers - hot	−1	0.5 to 1	35 to 40	no	no	10	+2-3	6 to 8	9 to 10
potatos (tubers)	−2 to 4	7 to 15	30	no	no	no	no	no	10 to 16
radish - summer	−4 to 6	0.5 to 1	7 to 8	7	4	no	no	no	3 to 4
radish - winter	−3 to 4	0.5 to 1	10	2 to 3	8	no	no	no	6 to 9
rhubarb (crowns)	no	5 to 8	90	no	no	no	no	no	no
rutabaga (Swede)	+4	1 to 2	20 to 25	no	no	7 to 8	−4	3 to 4	12 to 13
spinich	−5 to 7	2 to 3	15	2	7	7 to 12	−3-6	4 to 6	6 to 7
squash (summer) - zucchini	0	2.5 to 5	60	no	no	1	+3-4	4	7 to 10
sweet corn - early	−2 to 4	3 to 6	45	3	9 to 10	2	+2-3	4	9 to 14
sweet corn - mid-season	−2 to 3	3 to 6	45	3	10 to 11	2	+2-3	4	9 to 14
sweet corn - late	−2 to 3	3 to 6	45	no	no	2	+2-3	4	9 to 14
swiss chard	−2 to 4	1 to 2.5	20	2 to 3	9	7 to 8	−3-4	4	7 to 9
tomatoes - bush	0	1 to 1.5	60	no	no	6 to 8	+3-4	6 to 10	8 to 10
tomatoes - cherry	0	1 to 1.5	45	no	no	6 to 8	+3-4	6 to 10	8 to 9
turnip	−4 to 6	0.5 to 1.5	15	3 to 4	8	7 to 8	−4	3 to 4	5 to 8

* before (or after) last frost of spring   ** last successional sowing before first frost of winter   *** at harvest

OTHER HOMEWORLD TITLES

ATTRACTING BIRDS

ISBN 0-919433-87-1   64 pp.   5 1/2 x 8 1/2 $6.95

HERBS

ISBN 0-919433-99-5   64 pp.   5 1/2 x 8 1/2 $6.95

JAMS AND JELLIES

ISBN 0-919433-90-1   48 pp.   5 1/2 x 8 1/2 $4.95

PICKLES AND PRESERVES

ISBN 0-919433-88-X   48 pp.   5 1/2 x 8 1/2 $4.95

AVAILABLE IN OCTOBER, 1992

BREADMAKING

ISBN 1-551050016-1   64 pp.   5 1/2 x 8 1/2 $6.95

CHRISTMAS SURVIVAL GUIDE

ISBN 1-55105-019-6   64 pp.   5 1/2 x 8 1/2 $6.95

SINGLES' SURVIVAL GUIDE

ISBN 1-55105-018-8   64 pp.   5 1/2 x 8 1/2 $6.95

FURNITURE REFINISHING

ISBN 1-55105-022-6   64 pp.   5 1/2 x 8 1/2 $6.95

Look for these and other Lone Pine books at your local bookstore. If they're unavailable, order direct from:

Lone Pine Publishing
#206 10426-81 Avenue
Edmonton, Alberta   T6E 1X5
Phone: (403) 433-9333   Fax: (403) 433-9646